134567

D1581718

BASKET

FULL FLIGHT

Badger Publishing Limited
Oldmedow Road,
Hardwick Industrial Estate,
King's Lynn PE30 4JJ
Telephone: 01438 791037

www.badgerlearning.co.uk

2 4 6 8 10 9 7 5 3 1

Basketball ISBN 978-1-85880-383-8 (second edition) 2013

Publisher: Susan Ross
Senior Editor: Danny Pearson
Designer: Fiona Grant

Photos: Cover image: Aflo / Rex Features
Page 5: KeystoneUSA-ZUMA / Rex Features
Page 6: West Coast Surfer / Mood Board / Rex Features
Page 9: ZUMA / Rex Features
Page 10: KeystoneUSA-ZUMA / Rex Features
Page 12: Image Source / Rex Features
Page 14: Canadian Press / Rex Features
Page 16: John Raoux/AP/Press Association Images
Page 17: Michael Perez/AP/Press Association Images
Page 18: Julie Jacobson/AP/Press Association Images
Page 19: J Pat Carter/AP/Press Association Images
Page 23: Armando Arorizo/Zuma Press/Press Association Images
Page 25: KeystoneUSA-ZUMA / Rex Features
Page 27: CHINE NOUVELLE/SIPA / Rex Features
Page 29: Gregory Smith/AP/Press Association Images
Page 31: JOHN SWART/AP/Press Association Images

Attempts to contact all copyright holders have been made.
If any omitted would care to contact Badger Learning, we will be
happy to make appropriate arrangements.

BASKETBALL

Contents

1.	In the zone	4
2.	The court	6
3.	Basketball rules, okay?	8
4.	All for one	10
5.	Wheelchair basketball	12
6.	Coaching clinic	14
7.	Back to the roots	20
8.	Simply the best	21
9.	Women's basketball	24
10.	All around the world	26
11.	Hall of fame	28
12.	Nowhere I'd rather be...	30
Index		32

Badger
LEARNING

1. IN THE ZONE

Basketball is the top indoor sport in the world.

Players must focus every second they are on court. You're 'in the zone', totally at one with the game, or you're nowhere.

Picture a top basketball match. The indoor stadium is packed with noisy fans. On the brightly lit court, two teams play for glory.

There are ten players on court (five from each team). They pass the ball with skill and pace. Everyone is thinking fast and working for their team. There are seconds to play and the scores are even. The coaches prowl the side of the court like caged animals. Then one leaps into the air.

A power play from the team has ended with a shot on target. The ball spins round the hoop and falls into the basket. It's a last second winner. The crowd go wild.

This is the exciting world of basketball.

WELCOME TO LIFE IN THE ZONE

2. THE COURT

There is a basket with a backboard at either end of the court. The baskets are 46cm wide and three metres above the ground. A white net hangs from each basket.

The area under the basket is known as the key. Some of the hottest action takes place here.

There is a line through a circle at the end of the key. Free shots, awarded for fouls, are taken from here. Each shot on target scores one point.

There is a semi-circle outside the key. If you hit the basket with a shot inside the semi-circle, you score two points. Score from outside the line and it's three points.

Most courts are 25 metres long and 15 metres wide. That's not a big area for ten players and two match officials. Most of the players are well over two metres tall!

3. BASKETBALL RULES, OKAY?

Basketball rules can fill a book.
They can also change for men and
women, different age groups, and
for professional leagues like
America's NBA.

So, let's stick to the basics. Okay?

Basketball teams usually have ten
players. That's five on the court and
five substitutes. Unlike football, the
team coaches can use substitutes as
many times as they like.

Matches are played in four 10 minute
periods. These are known as quarters.

Every time the ball goes out of play,
the clock stops. So matches actually
last much longer than 40 minutes.

If the scores are level at full time, the
teams play an extra five minutes.
If the match is still tied at the end of
extra time, another five minutes must
be played. The teams keep playing
until there is a winner.

There is no such thing as a draw
in basketball.

4. ALL FOR ONE

Team spirit is a big thing in many sports, but in basketball it's vital.

Roger Neuss was a senior coach with England Basketball. He knows what it's like to be at the heart of a top match. When the pressure is on, it's all for one!

"Coaches and their players should work hard on set plays before every match," Roger explains. "That's when they plan how they are going to attack and defend. The players must know what they have to do out there on court. You have to keep thinking hard all the time.

"Basketball is all about team work. Every player is important. When all five players on court click as one, it's really something special."

5. WHEELCHAIR BASKETBALL

Wheelchair basketball was first played in the 1940s.

It originally started out as a way to help soldiers, who were in wheelchairs, to get good exercise. It quickly became a sport and it is now played in over 80 countries.

Wheelchair basketball is one of the biggest Paralympic events. Many teams take part in it from all over the world. The London 2012 Paralympics included teams from Great Britain, Australia, Germany, Italy, Japan, Mexico and the USA.

Wheelchair basketball was at the first Paralympic Games in 1960.

The rules are almost the same as basketball:
- The court is the same size.
- The basket is at the same height.
- There are ten players on court (five from each team).
- The scoring is identical.

Players are able to move the ball around the court by passing or dribbling.

They are required to throw or bounce the ball after every two pushes of the wheels on their chairs.

6. COACHING CLINIC

There are over 300 million basketball players in the world. And they all need to have the skills we are going to show you now.

LOOK RIGHT - PLAY RIGHT

Basketball players wear a vest, shorts and socks. Make sure these fit well and give you freedom to turn and move.

Basketball boots and shoes must have a good sole to give you grip on the court. Keep your footwear laced to protect your feet and ankles.

Ask your coach to look after any jewellery you may have. Don't wear them on court – you could hurt someone.

PASSING

- Focus on where the ball is going.
- Pass with power using two hands.
- Concentrate hard. Make your pass count.

SHOOTING (JUMP SHOT)

- Eyes focus just above the rim of the basket.
- Jump with your elbow in.
- Shoot the ball into the basket. Fingertips touch the ball last.

SHOOTING (LAY-UPS)

- Run at the net from an angle.
- Jump off your left foot for a right-handed lay-up.
- Rebound the ball off the backboard into the net.

DRIBBLING

- Look around the court, not at the ball.
- Keep your head up.
- Use either hand to move the ball.
- Protect the ball with your body and other arm.

TOP TIPS - OFFENCE

- Don't stand still on court. Move, change direction, change speed.
- Always be ready to take a pass.
- Only shoot when you have a good chance of scoring.
- Don't give the ball away.

TOP TIPS - DEFENCE

- Keep between the player you are marking and your basket.

- Keep your hands up.

- Be ready to cut out a bad pass and take the ball.

- When the other team shoots at the basket, be ready to jump for the rebound.

7. BACK TO THE ROOTS

Basketball was invented in the USA over 100 years ago.

A sports teacher called Dr James Naismith came up with the idea. He wanted an indoor game students could play in the school gym when it was snowy outside.

He hung peach baskets at the two ends of the gym. He gave his students a football to throw around. Basketball was born.

The first proper game took place on 21st December 1891. All the players were men. By the early 1900s, lots of women were playing too.

8. SIMPLY THE BEST

America's professional basketball league, the NBA, is simply the best in the world.

The NBA began in 1946. It now has 30 teams. There are two conferences with 15 teams each. There are five in each of three divisions within each conference.

The winners from the west and east meet in a series of play-off games to decide who will become NBA champions.

The best teams in recent years have been the Miami Heat and the Los Angeles Lakers.

The Los Angeles Lakers won three titles in a row in the early 00s.

Back then the team's best players were Kobe Bryant and Shaquille O'Neal. Kobe scored 81 points in one game; Shaquille scored 46 in another.

Other famous teams include the Chicago Bulls, Boston Celtics, New York Knicks, Orlando Magic and Utah Jazz.

Players from all over the world now star in the NBA. Matches are played in huge indoor stadiums. Every game is shown on TV. Top players earn millions of dollars every year. Sales of NBA sports goods top one billion dollars a year.

Shaquille O'Neal

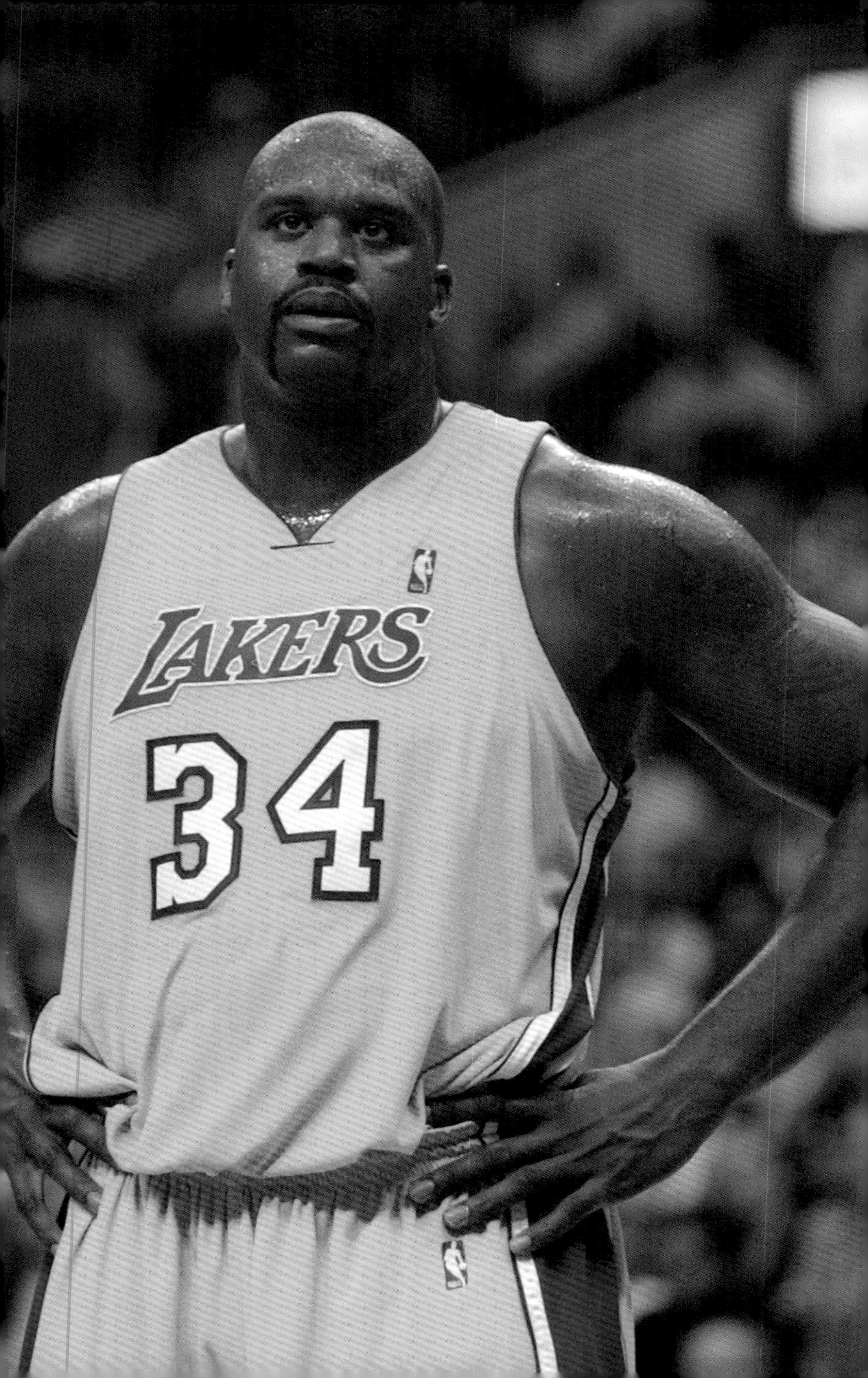
LAKERS
34

9. WOMEN'S BASKETBALL

More women are playing basketball now than ever before.

They have their own professional league in the USA, called the WNBA. This started in 1997. Like the NBA, it is split into teams from the west and east of the country.

There are 12 teams in the WNBA and the league runs through the summer.

Some critics have looked down on women's basketball over the years. But the arrival of the WNBA changed all that.

Now fans can enjoy seeing the best women players in the world. They have skill, style and a fierce will to win.

Top teams like the Los Angeles Sparks and the Indiana Fever play in packed stadiums. Stars like Diana Taurasi and Candace Parker get sacks of fan mail.

WOMEN'S BASKETBALL IS BIG NEWS

10. ALL AROUND THE WORLD

Basketball was born in the USA.
Now it is enjoyed all around the world.

Men's basketball teams in the 2012
Olympic Games in London included
Australia, Spain, China, Russia, France
and the USA. The USA won the gold
medal at the Games, but the other
countries are catching up fast.

Women's basketball joined the Olympics
in 1976. In 2012, top teams included
Australia, Brazil, the USA, France, Russia,
China, Turkey and Canada.

The Australian and French women's teams
show how teams around the world are
catching up.

The USA won gold again at the 2012
Olympics, but the Australians won the
bronze medal, and the French won the
silver medal.

Men and women also have their own
World Championships, which take place
every four years.

11. HALL OF FAME

The Basketball Hall of Fame is filled with the names of great players. Here are ten of the best:

1. Michael Jordan. A legend. Scored thousands of points for the Chicago Bulls.

2. Kareem Abdul-Jabbar. The NBA's all-time top scorer, with 38,387 points. Played for Los Angeles Lakers until he was 42.

3. Julius Erving. Best known for the way he could jump high above the basket and 'slam dunk' shots down through the rim.

4. 'Magic' Johnson. A hero for the Los Angeles Lakers. Famous for his smile on court. He loved playing basketball.

5. Larry Bird. Boston Celtics star. Won gold with the USA at the 1992 Olympics.

6. Scottie Pippen. Formed a dynamic duo with Michael Jordan.

7. Yao Ming was the tallest player in the NBA. He is 7 feet 6 inches tall.

8. Bill Russell. Rated as the best defender ever.

9. Charles Barkley. Had great power and a real will to win.

10. Shaquille O'Neal. One of the biggest men to ever play in the NBA. Although he was big he could still move quickly.

12. NOWHERE I'D RATHER BE...

A game of basketball is being played every minute of every day of the year.

From Melbourne to Manchester, Tokyo to Toronto, players of all ages are enjoying the biggest indoor sport in the world.

It doesn't matter if you are playing in your school sports hall or in front of thousands of fans in the Olympic Games or NBA, the thrill is the same.

Your mind is buzzing. Your vest is wet with sweat, but you don't care.

You see your chance to shoot. The ball cuts through the air and into the hoop. You've scored and you feel the thrill.

Let's leave the last words to basketball legend, Michael Jordan. This is what he said when he was playing for the Chicago Bulls:

"When I'm out on court in the heat of a great match, there's nowhere I'd rather be..."

INDEX

Abdul-Jabbar, Kareem 28
Australia 12, 26-27
backboard 6, 17
Barkley, Charles 29
basket 5-7, 13, 16, 19-20, 28
Bird, Larry 28
boots 15
Boston Celtics 22, 28
Bryant, Kobe 22
Chicago Bulls 22, 28, 31
court 4, 6-8, 11, 13, 15, 18,
      28, 31
defence 19
dribbling 13, 18
Erving, Julius 28
Indiana Fever 25
Johnson, 'Magic' 28
Jordan, Michael 28, 31
jump shot 16
key, the 7
lay-ups 17
Los Angeles Lakers 21, 28-29
Los Angeles Sparks 25
Ming, Yao 29

Naismith, Dr James 20
NBA 8, 21-22, 24, 28-30
Neuss, Roger 11
New York Knicks 22
offence 18
Olympic Games 26-28, 30
O'Neal, Shaquille 22-23, 29
Orlando Magic 22
Parker, Candace 25
passing 13, 16
Pippen, Scottie 28
quarters 8
Russell, Bill 29
shooting 16-17
shorts 15
substitutes 8
Taurasi, Diana 25
Utah Jazz 22
vest 15, 30
WNBA 24